Published 2007 by Tangent Books
3 Monmouth Place
Bath BA1 2AT
Tel: 01225 463983
www.tangentbooks.co.uk
E-mail: hello@tangentbooks.co.uk

For Miranda and Oliver

Publisher: Richard Jones
Production: Anne Smith, Steve Faragher
Design: Joe Burt, Trevor Wyatt

Thanks to:
Leonie Campbell-King and Dayna Stevens

James Russell has asserted his right under the Copyright, Designs and
Patents Act of 1988 to be indentified as the author of this work.

Øivind Høvland has asserted his right under the Copyright, Designs and
Patents Act of 1988 to be indentified as the illustrator of this work.

HOW TO
TURN YOUR PARENTS
GREEN

BY

JAMES RUSSELL

Illustrations by Øivind Hovland

THIS BOOK **BELONGS** TO:

....

....

CONTENTS

The weather's gone weird. The polar bears are anxious. Ghastly Global Warming is here. Every day there's some new thing to worry about, but don't panic. Help is at hand. Yes, someone's about to save the planet and guess what? It's you.

Only you can do it, because only you can make the culprits change their ways. Only you can nag, pester, bug, torment and punish the people who are merrily wrecking your world. And who are they? Who cranks the heating up so you can't breathe? Who drives everywhere? Who chucks out mountains of Revolting Rubbish? You? Your friends?

Meet the Groans. They grumble and gripe about traffic and heating bills, but grown-ups have got us into this mess and they're too busy goggling at the TV and booking exotic holidays to sort it out. Only you can make the Groans behave because only you can make their lives a misery if they don't. We'll help you draw up a Glorious Green Charter for them to sign, and show you how to punish them – oh yes – if they don't change their Grumbelicious ways. Don't be an Eco-Worrier, be an Eco-Warrior. And turn your parents Green.

1

GLORIOUS GREEN CHARTER

I do solemnly attest and vow that I care deeply about the future of my children and my children's children, not to mention my children's children's children[+]. I do not wish for them to be subjected to the perils of a new Ice Age, nor am I desirous that they should be forced to evolve into aquatic organisms in order to contend with rising sea levels.

I accept that my brilliantly talented children understand way more about this So-Called Global Warming Nonsense than I do, and so I am prepared to accept, utterly and unconditionally, their plan for a Glorious Green Future.

And knowing that I never do anything unless I know it will cost me if I don't, I accept the system of punitive fines to be levied and collected by ...., Guardian of the Glorious Green Future, in the unlikely event of my failure to GET MY FINGER OUT AND CHANGE MY GROANY GRUMBELICIOUS WAYS*.

+Up to you how far you go here.
Some Groans have very short attention spans.

You can leave this bit out if you think it's too controversial. What does 'Get your finger out' mean anyway? Is it like pulling your socks up? Where's the finger in the first place???

Signed ....

Parent|Carer|Teacher (delete as applicable)

APPROVED

CHAPTER 1

OH HORRORS! IT'S GHASTLY
GLOBAL WARMING

t's horrible and it's happening. The world is hotting up. It's enough to make you dive back into bed and hide under the covers. But don't be an Eco-Worrier, be an Eco-Warrior. The planet needs saving and you – yes, YOU – are going to save it.

Who, you're asking? Me? What can I do?

Go charging around the ocean in an inflatable dinghy, saving whales and chaining yourself to oil rigs like those grizzled Greenpeace veterans? Perhaps not.

Invent a marvellous machine that gobbles up carbon dioxide and turns it into double choc chunk chip ice cream? Doubtful.

Persuade people in Brazil and Indonesia to stop cutting down all those trees FOR HEAVEN'S SAKE and take up origami instead? Maybe next week...

Ask your parents very nicely to demonstrate their support for your future by signing the Charter you're about to draw up, and by doing what it says? What?

Think about this for a moment: You know that Ghastly Global Warming is caused by people pumping Gruesome Greenhouse Gases into the atmosphere? Of course you do. And you know that the most important of these is carbon dioxide (CO_2), which is what you get when you burn things that contain carbon? I'm sure you know that too.

Can you guess how much CO_2 we humans release into the atmosphere every day?

1. A bit.

2. Quite a lot.

3. 70 million tonnes.

OK, so that was dead easy, but if you bear in mind that CO_2 is as light as air, that's an awful lot of gas. Here's a more difficult one.

Do you know which of the following activities DOESN'T produce CO_2?

1. Running to school because you've been wandering along worrying about how peculiar the weather's been lately and you have suddenly noticed that it's VERY QUIET?

7

2. Eating your favourite juicy apple that has a tiny label on it saying, or rather whispering, Product of Chile?

3. Blowing leaves around the garden with Dad's Macho Leaf Blowing Bazooka-Type Thing?

4. Farting.

Answer: 4. *We breathe out CO_2. Transporting fruit means burning fuel, which produces CO_2. A leaf blower uses electricity, which mostly comes from burning oil or gas, which produces CO_2. A fart is mostly methane, which would be great news for baked bean munchers if methane wasn't also a Gruesome Greenhouse Gas.*

So we've got that straight. The question is: whose fault is it that CO_2 is blowing up like a huge duvet round the earth and making the weather go weird? Yours? Who's been wasting the Earth's resources for years and driving everywhere because they're too lazy to walk? You? Or the Grumbling Groans?

You know who I mean. They grumble about the unseasonal weather and they groan about having to recycle. They moan that organic carrots are too expensive and they have a big shouty tantrum if anyone says they shouldn't fly off on another holiday.

You'll find Groans in the classroom and Groans at

the shops, but the best place to spot a Groan is at home. Here's one now: he's slumped in front of the TV, moaning about the draught and shouting for someone to turn the heat up. And here's another one in the kitchen, salivating over a holiday brochure and complaining that the supermarkets have run out of her favourite Peruvian blueberries.

THE YEARS **1980–2000** WERE THE HOTTEST IN FOUR HUNDRED YEARS.

Yes, those Grumbly Grimbly Groans are everywhere and they're wrecking your world. It's time to do something about it – it's time to turn them Green. So here's the plan: You can get them to sign the Charter on p2. Or get a nice clean piece of paper – recycled, of course – and write out the Charter, making it look as important as possible. Remember, to a Groan, appearances are everything.

Now, to Save the Planet!
Hurry up, it's nearly tea time.

YOU ARE THE PLANET!

THE PLANET IS YOU!

CHAPTER 2

YOU ARE THE PLANET! THE PLANET IS YOU!

So where would you find Nature?

1. Over in Africa, or out in the countryside somewhere, maybe in Wales.

2. Everywhere.

3. On the telly, hosted by David Attenborough or Bill Oddie or _____ (insert favourite naturalist).

Yes, Nature is everywhere. It's on the way to school. It's in the garden. It's crawling about on us, in the form of lice and other visitors. It's even inside us. We're all part of Nature and Nature is part of us. As Noah liked to say to his animal crew:

WE'RE ALL IN THE SAME BOAT

That's the way Groovy Greens see our relationship with the world around us. They understand that everything we do has an impact on the world, so we should think about how much energy we use, how much rubbish we throw away, and so on. Groans disagree, strongly. They do not like to go without. They don't like words like 'less'. They don't want one chocolate biscuit, they want the whole packet. They consider Greens to be Spoilsports and Party Poopers.

To a Groan there are only two important rules for living:

MORE, CHEAPER!
and
MAKE LIFE EASY!

The main aim of a Groan's life is to exploit as much of the planet as possible before someone else does. Even before Ghastly Global Warming, this philosophy was making the world a sadder place. Fiendish Fertilizers and Pestilential Pesticides have killed off wildflowers, birds, bees and hedgehogs. Our rivers and seas are horribly polluted. Most of us live surrounded by the noise, dirt and danger of traffic.

Groans think all this is fine and natural. So what if the hedgehog becomes extinct? So what if climate change kills millions of people? So what if kids have nowhere to play because there are too many cars?

People die, they say with a shrug. Species disappear. Kids can play computer games.

You do not have the freedom your parents had, never mind your grandparents. Can you play football in the road or ride your bike to school? Do you have places to hang out close to home? Is there anything beautiful where you live? Not so long ago children of all ages played outside, independently – the world was theirs. Why isn't it yours?

Groans argue that the world is just naturally the way it is, and that nothing you or I do can change it. They're wrong. Ordinary people made the world what it is and ordinary people can change it again. For Greens, life is a constant struggle against Groanish greed and stupidity, but every now and again they win.

THE WAR AGAINST DDT

In the 1960s biologists began to notice that birds were dying. In parts of England, they were actually dropping dead out of the sky, and it soon became obvious why: farmers were spraying a new kind of Insane Insecticide on their crops. This stuff, called DDT, was so deadly that it killed not only the insects but anything that ate insects, and also anything that ate the insect-eaters. Nobody knew exactly how the stuff worked, but they kept spraying it anyway.

An American biologist called Rachel Carson wrote a terrifying book called *Silent Spring*, which explained what was going on, and as a consequence, DDT and other Insane Insecticides were banned. If you hear a bird singing, spare a thought for Rachel Carson.

THE ARCTIC MAY BE ICE-FREE IN SUMMER BY 2040

THE BATTLE OF OZONE

In the 1920s Thomas Midgley invented a new kind of chemical compound: chlorofluorocarbons (CFCs) could be used in air conditioning units and fridges, and as aerosol spray propellants, so they Made Life Easy. But each time someone squirted deodorant under their arms the CFCs went floating off into the atmosphere. In the 1970s scientists discovered that this rapidly growing cloud of CFCs was doing Terrible Things to a layer of gas called ozone.

The Ozone Layer stops dangerous solar rays reaching the earth, so when a huge hole was discovered over Antarctica – caused by all these nasty chemicals – the world decided to take action. And it really did. CFCs were banned in many countries and production finally stopped in 1996.

By 2003 scientists were smiling: the rate of ozone

depletion was slowing, and the process of repair
– predicted to take fifty years or more – was underway.

Which just shows that things can change. We can
tackle Ghastly Global Warming. **And you, yes YOU,
can turn those parents Green.**

This world is your inheritance. Those are your beaches
that will disappear if the sea level rises. They're your
frogs and your larks and your bumblebees and your
hedgehogs. The rainforests are yours, and so are the
orangutans and the gorillas – not yours to own, but
yours to enjoy, and yours to look after.

So where do we start?

INTRODUCING... THE ENFORCER

So you've explained to those parents what needs to be done, but suppose they don't do it. Are you going to let them get away with it? Of course not. You know Groans love the folding stuff (that's cash, not deck chairs), but how much do they love their money? Enough to change their Grumbelicious ways? There's only one way to find out, and as Guardian of the Glorious Green Future it's up to you to play Enforcer.

OFFENCE	FINE
Leaving lights on	20p per light
Using high-energy bulbs	10p per bulb
Thermostat over 20 deg	20p per degree
Not insulating water tank	50p per week
Leaving stuff on standby	20p per unit
Using non-rechargeable batteries	10p per battery/week
Late payment of fines	10 per cent of fine total

All weekly fines are payable by 7pm on Friday evening. Add 10 per cent if late.

THE INSTANT ECO-WARRIOR

CHAPTER 3

THE INSTANT
ECO-WARRIOR

**You want to save the planet? You do? Really?
Then try this:**

1. Find a light someone's left on.

2. Turn it off.

OK, that wasn't exactly fun, but every Smidgeon* of
energy we save means a bit less needs to be produced,
which means a bit less CO_2 in the sky. Most of our
heat and power comes from burning coal, gas or
oil, known as Fossil Fuels because they originated
as plants and animals that died millions of years
ago. Burning fossil fuels releases CO_2, which causes
Ghastly Global Warming.

* Less than a Hatful, more than a Nip.

To stop the world turning into a giant sauna, we have three choices:

1. Use less energy.

2. Get energy from nuclear power, which doesn't involve carbon.

3. Get energy from somewhere else.

Naturally, your average Groan isn't keen on No. 1. Groans love to use Hatfuls of energy, so long as it's not their own. They love giant fridges, huge TVs, power showers with nozzles that fire jets of water in every direction. They're always desperately in need of more electrical sockets to plug in their blenders and toasted sandwich makers and cappuccino machines and flat-screen TVs and all the rest of our energy-guzzling gismology. They crank up the thermostat until everyone's overcome with heat exhaustion, and light up the neighbourhood with their Hellish Halogens.

Groans would quite happily pump CO_2 into the air until the cows float home, but they're also Nuts for Nuclear. Well, next time you hear them blathering on about how we need to build more nuclear power stations so we don't have to buy gas from those Russians, why not test their knowledge...

Nuclear Power Quiz

1. When a reactor exploded at the Chernobyl nuclear power station, Ukraine, in 1986, how far did the radioactivity travel: **a.** 10 miles? **b.** 100 miles? **c.** 1,000 miles and more?

2. Oldbury nuclear power station stops generating in 2008, after 40 years of service. Guess when it will finally close: **a.** 2028? **b.** 2118? **c.** 2068?

3. Nuclear waste is lethally poisonous for centuries. So what do people do with it? **a.** There isn't any, silly! **b.** Bury it in a hole? **c.** Recycle it?

Answers: 1c. British fields were contaminated, and radioactivity was detected in the USA; **2b.** Yes, really. **3b.** Need I say more?

The thing is, we could cut our energy use by a third quite easily, and the best place to start is at home.

Which of these best describes your house in the winter?

TURN DOWN YOUR THERMOSTAT BY 1°C AND YOU COULD CUT YOUR FUEL BILLS BY

10%

1. The roof is covered in contented parrots, soaking up the warmth of the tiles.

2. Your Dad's sitting on the sofa in a T-shirt, watching footie on TV and munching chocolate biscuits.

3. Scraps of paper, socks and younger children blow about the place even when all the windows and doors are shut.

4. The boiler sounds as if it might just explode at any moment.

5. For every person in the house, seventeen light bulbs are blazing.

Suggestions: 1. Time for some loft insulation. **2.** Turn the thermostat down and wait. **3.** Get draught excluding stuff. **4.** If the boiler's older than you, it's munching money and energy. **5.** Replace bulbs with low-energy ones and switch off ones you're not using.

THE LAZY TRAIN TO CHUBVILLE

It's all over the news – we're becoming a nation of Telly Tubbies. Well, what do you expect if people always use energy that isn't their own? With a machine for every job, we're less and less active, but we guzzle more and more goodies. The result? We're on the Lazy Train to Chubville.

Look at Dad. He's obviously been enjoying some festive cheer. Now he doesn't feel too great. His feet are cold because his blood scarcely reaches them, so he demands more heat and chomps another packet of chocolate digestives. Viruses and germs leap aboard and meet no resistance. If Dad were in a zoo, the RSPCA would close it down.

Green Dad keeps trim by raking leaves, walking to the shops, riding a bike to work and protesting about Airport Expansion. His heart pumps happily, so his feet are warm and he doesn't need the heating on. He's a happy organism. He's Green!

Excellent Energy Saving Ideas

1. Have a 'No Power' day. Yes, apart from the freezer and other essentials, turn the power off for twenty-four hours. No lights. No TV. No computer.

2. Dance. If the weather's too nasty for outdoor fun, have a disco in the kitchen. Or form a family band: rattle those pans! Strut your stuff! Kick up a racket! If anyone complains, tell them you're doing it for the Planet (man).

3. Keep the heating at 20 degrees or below and turn it off at night.

Meet Micro Jen

Micro Jen is small but tough.
Micro Jen is very Green.
Micro Jen makes electricity At Home.

People are already doing it, and soon everyone will generate their own electricity from Renewable Sources:

1. Sizzling Solar captures the sun's energy in roof panels.

2. Wondrous Wind Turbines harness the power of – you guessed it – the wind.

3. Marvellous Microhydro takes energy from rivers and streams.

Once operating, none of these produces CO_2 or any other kind of waste, and if you produce more electricity than you need, you can sell it!

But if the Parents find all this a bit daunting, you can still get your energy from the sun and the wind – there are loads of Green power companies out there, and you can buy it from them.

Pedalling for the Planet

Q. How do watch TV and keep fit at the same time?

A. Pedal power.

Very soon, you'll be able to buy a pedal-powered generator to drive your TV, which means it's Farewell, Telly Tubby, and Hello, Vigorous Viewer. All-Night Gogglers will sport bulging calf muscles. You'll be able to pedal your washing machine too, plus computers, power tools, etc.

THE CRAZY TRUTH ABOUT BATTERIES

How many batteries do you have in the house? When you add up phones, games, cameras, etc, you may find quite a few, and each one is a Groanish nightmare of waste.

Battery facts

1. Batteries may contain lead, mercury, cadmium and other poisonous metals.

2. A non-rechargeable battery can take up to 50 times more energy to make than it provides in its lifetime.

3. Listening to an MP3 player or talking on the phone as you walk is a good way of getting run over.

ON STANDBY – FOR WHAT?

Once upon a time, a TV was either On or Off. Then someone invented Standby and now TVs and all our other appliances burn energy twenty-four hours a day, wasting millions of pounds a year*. But for what? Surely a TV which is Off is just as ready for action as a TV on Standby – all you have to do is push a button, for Heaven's Sake. It's not as if the TV is going to leap up at a moment's notice and do something heroic. It doesn't need to be Prepared for Anything. It's a telly, not a firefighter.

* A TV on standby uses as much energy as a DVD player when it's playing.

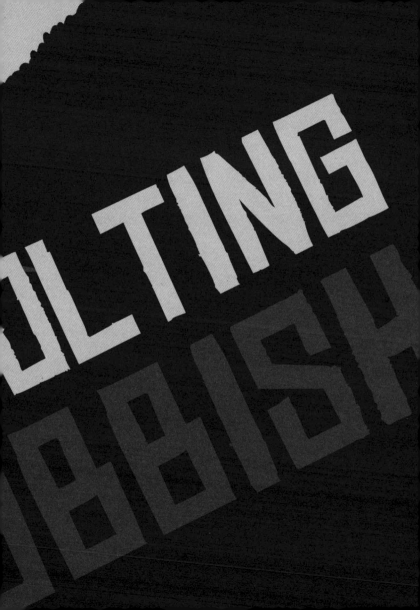

CHAPTER 4

REVOLTING RUBBISH

L andfill sounds quite useful, doesn't it?

Groan 1: "Oh no, there's a gap in our land. I wish we had something to put in it."

Groan 2: "Don't worry, here's fifty million tonnes of disgusting nappies, plastic bags, rotting food and other stuff to fill it up with! And – at no extra cost – a load of nasty methane gas and poisonous leachates!"

Groan 1: "Great! What's a leachate?"

Groan 2: "It's like a smoothie made of all the horrible smelly sludgy stuff that leaks out of the rubbish, mixed with rainwater. It pollutes the water table and gets into rivers and streams!"

Groans think that future generations will admire them for their motorways and tall buildings, but their legacy to the world is rubbish: huge, revolting mountains of the stuff.

Fifty years ago, no one threw anything away unless they absolutely had to, but now Groans are constantly chucking out old computers and tellies, binning everything from plastic packaging to last night's leftovers. Never in the history of the world have people created rubbish like our Groans. Now they've filled up most of the quarries in Britain and they're having to load their old junk on ships and take it off to India and other places.

OVER CHRISTMAS WE WILL THROW AWAY ENOUGH WRAPPING PAPER TO COVER GUERNSEY*

*13 billion plastic carrier bags are used in the UK each year.

Of course they moan about higher Council Tax bills, but they also whinge when you mention recycling. What? Put our cans in a separate bin? Have you ANY IDEA how hard that is?

In Germany, you have to recycle, and if you don't you're likely to get a visit from the Rubbish Inspectors. Within five years the same thing will be happening here, so you might as well train your Groans now.

MEET AL

It isn't very shrewd to bin an aluminium can. If you collect a hundred cans and melt them down, you can make ninety-nine and a half new cans, and only use 5% of the energy needed to make them from scratch. To make aluminium in the first place, you mine bauxite, which is done by ripping big holes in rainforests, then you use crazy quantities of electricity to make the stuff into aluminium. It's a ghastly business, but once Al emerges from the fiery furnace he's practically immortal – so long as you don't chuck your cans in the dustbin.

MEET POLLY

Groans adore Polly Thene because she Makes Life Easy, but Polly is not a Friend of the Earth. Take sandwich bags: first, you have to pump up a load of oil, stick it on a huge leaky tanker and take it to a plastics factory. There, you manipulate molecules and whatnot, and Hey Presto!, there are boxes of sandwich bags heading for the supermarket, where your Mum buys them.

She bags up your sandwich and sends you off to school. Four hours later, you remove the sandwich from the bag, eat the sandwich and conscientiously throw the bag away. It goes from bin to bin, until the rubbish men pick it up and take it to the nearby landfill site. And in it goes. And stays there. For about five hundred years. That's four hours of use for half a millennium of pollution! What an absolutely brilliant scheme! Not. And guess what? Here in Britain we 'use' about five million plastic bags a day.

And in countries where the people aren't quite as Neat and Tidy as us, Polly Thene is getting everywhere. In Rwanda, for instance, farmland is being covered by a layer of plastic. Do crops grow well in plastic? Do cows and pigs thrive on a diet of plastic? Not exactly. Meanwhile, the oceans of the world are filling up with plastic bags. Do whales and dolphins see the stuff bobbing about and think 'Oh Joy! It's Polly Thene!"

Greens are starting to persuade Groans everywhere, from Uganda to Devon, that plastic bags are not a very good invention, but naturally Groans are resistant. Why give up something so convenient, just because the world is rapidly being buried under an indestructible layer of plastic? The truth is:

A plastic bag is just LANDFILL waiting to happen.

The same is true of plastic bottles. You can recycle these, but it isn't that easy. Until about thirty years ago, nobody bought water in plastic bottles. People in that far-off time used to get a glass of water from the tap and if they were going out they had a drink before they left. It's not as if we live in the Sahara Desert is it? OK, if you really think you can't make it to the shops and back without keeling over from the effects of dehydration, invest in a washable flask – they are next year's iPod!

Time to show Polly the door

1. Find a stylish cloth or string bag and buy at least ten, then stash them by the front door, in the car and anywhere else you can think of.

2. Try out different ways of transporting sandwiches – put them in a Tupperware-type container (TTC) or wrap in a napkin.

3. Buy fruit and veg in paper bags, if available, or put them loose in a basket.

4. Avoid clingfilm at all costs. Use a TTC for leftovers.

Recycling tips

1. Set up a system, e.g. a container under the sink for cans, etc. Remember: Groans like things to be Neat and Tidy.

2. Call the Council and order extra black bins. That way you have one for paper, one for glass and one for metal.

3. Rinse jars, bottles, etc and put in glass container.

4. Rinse cans and tins, and put in metal container.

5. Put paper in paper container.

Not too hard so far, is it?

6. Put yucky food waste (anything cooked, old bread, meat, citrus peels) in the brown bin, and put cardboard beside it – if you don't have one, call your Council and tell them to GET ON THE STICK!

7. Make some Cool Compost (see How to Turn your Garden Green, Chapter Eight, p64).

8. Stash hazardous things (batteries, dead computers, garden chemicals you're getting rid of) and ask the Council what to do with them.

9. Get milk delivered (your milkman will use those glass bottles up 30 times, then they get recycled).

10. Get water from the tap. A little louder? GET WATER FROM THE TAP!!!

You, yes YOU! are your household's Rubbish Inspector. It's your job to inspect recycling bins and the wheelie bin and take action for Improper Disposal, with a fine of 20p per item. Old sandwich in the wheelie? 20p. Polly in the food bin? 20p. Al in the wheelie? 20p, plus a slap round the head with a wet fish.

GO ZERO

If you want to be a Superhero of Rubbish, then try to
Go Zero. It's very simple, you just don't throw anything
away. I don't mean leave your rubbish mouldering and
stinking up the kitchen. You just don't make rubbish.
Not any. None. How do you do it? Start with items
1 to 10 above. What's left? Packaging, mostly. And
there's a great way to deal with packaging: leave it
at the shop.

THE RUBBISH INSPECTOR!

Sometimes you have to be cruel (sorry, Groans) to be kind (to the planet), and as the Rubbish Inspector, it's your job to inspect all bins and take action for Improper Disposal. Don't be tempted to take on the job of sorting rubbish. What will happen when you leave home? They need to be fully trained by then or they'll be tossing it all in the wheelie as soon as your back is turned. If you catch them binning stuff that should be recycled, make them do it properly and issue an on-the-spot fine..

ITEM NOT RECYCLED	FINE
Glass bottle and jars	20p per item
Plastic containers	20p per item
Paper	20p per offence
Tins	20p per item
Cardboard	20p per offence
Cooked food waste	20p per offence
Compostable waste (peelings etc)	20p per offence

Fines are all on-the-spot.

37

WATCH OUT WATER WASTERS!

CHAPTER 5

WATCH OUT
WATER WASTERS!

Phew, well at least we don't have to worry about water, I say, running the tap to brush my teeth. We've got so much of the stuff we don't know what to do with it!

If only life were that simple. With our washing machines and multi-nozzle power showers and baths you could wash a cow in, we're sucking more and more water from reservoirs and rivers.

And there's a lot more to water than just water. Uh? I mean the actual H2O is only part of the story. By the time water lands on my toothbrush it's been filtered and purified, tested and pumped, and at each stage energy has been used.

So I'm brushing away and the clean water is running down the sink, and this clean water goes into the drain and into the sewage system with all the Nasty Business we don't like to think about, and off it goes to be filtered and purified and tested and pumped, all over again. If it rains heavily, the sewers overflow and the Nasty Stuff escapes into rivers and streams, and if there are bad floods people's houses fill up with disgusting sewagey water.

WHEN CLEAN IS DIRTY

Most modern cleaning products are not clean. They may remove grub and grease from your kitchen counters (and from you) but they're full of Terrible Toxins, and these Terrible Toxins either go down the sink or into the bin and from there to a Loathsome Landfill Site near you. When Groans squirt germ killing spray all over the kitchen, they're poisoning the air you breathe – that's why the stuff stinks.

But, Groans protest, we must fight germs! Germs are the Great Enemy! Are they really? In fact, we live surrounded by Germs – our bodies are full of them. We just need to keep particularly hideous ones at bay, and the best way of doing that is to have clean hands and handle food properly.

Any chemicals you use will linger and build up in your carpets and furniture. If they go down the drain they can leak out through cracked pipes or when it rains hard enough to make the drains overflow, and then the Terrible Toxins go to work on Mother Nature.

DREADFUL DRAINS

Horrid hair and slimy soapscum sometimes combine to create a revolting blockage in your bathroom sink, so what do you do? Buy a bottle of hideous acid to dissolve it? Or unscrew the U-bend and clean it out? Yes, the chemical option Makes Life Easy, but unscrewing the U-bend means saving the waterworks from processing another dose of poisoned water.

BEASTLY BLEACH

Bleach stinks because it contains poisonous chlorine. For you chemists out there, the main ingredient is sodium hypochlorite, which is chlorine added to lye. Mix the stuff with ammonia or vinegar and you've got chlorine gas – not pleasant. Pour some into a river and you're likely to create organochlorines, which kill pretty much everything. Is this the kind of thing you want in the house? NO! Is it necessary to your health and welfare? NO! What should we do? GET RID OF IT!

So why, you're wondering, is your house full of poisonous stuff? Can you guess? Because chemical cleaning products Make Life Easy. They also add making the house Neat and Tidy into the bargain. The trouble is it's neat, tidy and awash in Terrible Toxins.

Poison Patrol, I mean Poisson Patrol, I mean... what?

USING A HOSE TO WASH YOUR CAR WASTES UP TO

30

BUCKETS OF WATER

1. List the Poissons: toilet cleaner, washing powder, bathroom cleanser*, things with names like He-Man.

2. Present the parents with the list, and give them a month to switch over to eco-friendly stuff and dispose of Poissons in a righteous manner.

3. Patrol again. Fine 50p per Poisson found.

*Like a cleaner, but sounds sort of religious

Use some old-fashioned cleaning materials (consult the internet for details): baking soda, vinegar, salt, lemon juice, vegetable oil, borax, washing soda, elbow grease.

The trouble with toilets

Guess how much of the water in a family house goes down the toilet?

1. A tenth.

2. A third.

3. An eighth.

Answer: 2. Yes, the old WC is a thirsty beast, so get the parents to think about fitting a low-flow version. In the meantime, bear in mind this advice on flushing etiquette, which comes from the deserts of the Southwestern USA:

> *If it's yellow, stay mellow*
> *If it's brown, flush it down*

Also, do you know how much toilet paper your family flushes away every year? It's easy to work out: just find out how much the parents buy. Chances are, no one's saving any for a special occasion. In any event, toilet paper must be recycled. Before use, obviously.

Watch out Water Wasters!

Time for some discipline. Water is precious, and wasting it isn't even fun.

1. Set depth limits on baths and time limits on showers, and fine transgressors 20p.

2. Check that washing machines and dishwashers are run on an Eco setting, so they use less heat and less water. 20p per infraction.

3. Use a watering can instead of a hose. 20p again

4.   Turn the tap off when you're brushing your teeth.

Leaving the tap running is one of the great Eco Crimes. How hard is it to switch a tap on and off? Instant fine of 20p, followed by tap turning lessons.

QUICK DRIP FIX

A dripping tap can fill a bath in one day. To fix: turn off water; unscrew tap; take out tap washer; replace with one you've remembered to buy beforehand; replace tap; switch on water. Time taken: two minutes. Cost: less than a pound.

Sensational Sewage!

Sewage may be nasty, but it isn't useless. These are some uses of sewage (spot the one I made up):

1.   Solids from sewage (yes, exactly what you think) are dried and burnt to generate electricity.

2.   If properly processed and used in the right conditions, sewage makes an excellent fertiliser, exactly like manure.

3.   Dried sewage is an essential ingredient of pipe and hand-rolling tobacco.

PESTER FOR THE

PLANET

CHAPTER 6

PESTER FOR THE PLANET!

You may have heard of Pester Power. It's the reason companies put adverts between your favourite TV shows. They're not expecting you to rush out and buy the latest PlayStation game or DVD, they're relying on you to bug your Groans until they buy stuff for you. And it works, doesn't it? Groans can't resist it, because deep down, they think that buying you stuff will make you happy.

Now imagine if every child in the country channelled their Pester Power in the service of the Glorious Green Future. Imagine if, instead of whining for DVDs, everyone griped and grumbled about organic carrots or environmentally friendly washing powder. You can change the way your parents shop, and that in turn will change the world. Pestering for the Planet! Remember, you read it here first.

BUY NOW, PAY LATER

Here's a question: If everything you ever bought had a little asterisk next to the price and some teeny tiny small print that said: 'Price subject to change after purchase', would you buy it? No way!

That's why retailers don't advertise it. Plus they don't have to. But we rarely get charged the full price for stuff when we buy it. We don't pay for the long term effects of Pestilential Pesticides or Fiendish Fertilizers, and we don't pay for the social costs of Cheap-not-Cheerful clothes or computers, and we certainly don't pay the full price for transport.

Your Mum might beam with pride when she fills a supermarket trolley for fifty quid, but who will be paying to clean up the countryside, deal with the mountains of Revolting Rubbish, not to mention all that CO_2 produced by flying blueberries (see p53)? Er... you will.

How to shop greenly

1. Take your own Sturdy Cloth Bags.

2. Avoid Pointless and Pernicious Packaging by

buying loose fruit and vegetables and disdaining processed food items.

3. Read labels. See where things come from. If your carrots are from Canada or your apples from Australia, think how far these poor fruit and veggies have travelled. Is it worth it? Couldn't you pay a little more for something less tired?

4. Even better, do some shopping at a farmers' market. Or get a veg box delivered. Or sign up for an allotment and Growing Your Own

5. Avoid Despicable Disposables: things like kitchen paper, paper plates and ready-made meals in a box are just landfill waiting to happen.

Cheap-not-cheerful cotton

So your Mum went to the supermarket and bought you three lovely cotton T-shirts for 49p. What a bargain! But why are they so cheap? Is it because:

1. The supermarket manager was feeling generous and paid for everything except the plastic bag?

2. In China, everything is just, like, Really Cheap? So people can buy cotton, make three T-shirts and

send them all the way over to your local T---s and still make a profit?

3. The T-shirts are made out of cotton grown and processed with absolutely no concern for the environment by people who are paid a pittance, even by their own dismal standards?

You guessed it, **3.** Cotton is a wonderful fabric but its manufacture causes endless misery. The populations of entire countries – kids included – are the virtual slaves of government-run cotton industries, and cotton is notoriously thirsty. Cotton plantations have reduced the famous Aral Sea in Central Asia to a polluted puddle. The solution? Buy organic.

THE TIGER'S TAIL

Groans have a thing about garden furniture. This is because:

1. They like sitting down.

2. They like the garden to be Neat and Tidy.

Of course, garden furniture is often made out of wood, but no Ghastly Garden Furniture salesman is going to admit that this wood may have been pillaged from ancient and valuable forests.

The Siberian Tiger has an unfortunate problem. Another species (Homo Groanus) has decided that the tiger's fur is more fun than its own boring skin. This wouldn't be so bad if the Siberian Tiger didn't also have a second problem. Being a big hungry carnivore it eats wild boar – though it would be better off chomping Groans – which get nice and fat eating Siberian acorns. The acorns in turn grow on Siberian oak trees, but the other species aforementioned thinks a beautiful wood like oak is wasted standing around as trees – it has a Destiny To Fulfil, as a matching set of table and four chairs, only £159.99 from your local store!

No oak means no boar, means hungry tiger wandering in search of food and encountering Horrible Hunters, means tiger losing his skin.

So it is up to you to make sure that your Groans only buy wood marked with the Forest Stewardship Council logo.

IF BLUEBERRIES WERE MEANT TO FLY, THEY'D HAVE WINGS

95% OF FRUIT EATEN IN THE UK IS IMPORTED

It's a small, round blue berry, hence its name. Does it have wings? Er, no. But this American fruit does have numerous relatives: cranberry, bilberry, cowberry (yes, really), sheepberry (OK, maybe not). And it has lots in common with other fruit such as blackcurrants and plums, which are disgustingly Good For You.

Plums grow like crazy in Britain, but nobody wants them. Blueberries don't grow here at all, and everybody loves them.

Welcome to the world of Groan logic. The thing is, plums are not cool. They don't come in neat little plastic containers (known as clamshells, though no self-respecting clam would be seen dead in one), and they have Unfortunate Associations: in their dried form (prunes) they have long been sold as a cure for constipation. Well, hello! Blueberries make you poo too.

The difference is blueberries travel thousands of miles by plane for the privilege, and people hoover them off the supermarket shelves, muttering about 'antioxidants' and 'supernutrients', even though each little fruit is doused in murderous quantities of Pestilential Pesticides.

So why not suggest to the Groans that they leave the blueberries on the shelf and preserve some plums instead? If they say something whingey like, "But I don't like plums, I like blueberries, they're so cute and tiny and blue," deliver your killer line:

If Blueberries were meant to fly, they'd have wings.

Three good reasons to go organic:

1. Organic farmers don't use Pestilential Pesticides or Fiendish Fertilisers, which means their food isn't covered in chemicals, which is good news for you.

2. Their land isn't covered in chemicals either, which is good news for plants and wildlife.

3. Organic farmers treat their animals well, and don't stuff them full of growth hormones, antibiotics and other horrors, which is just plain good news.

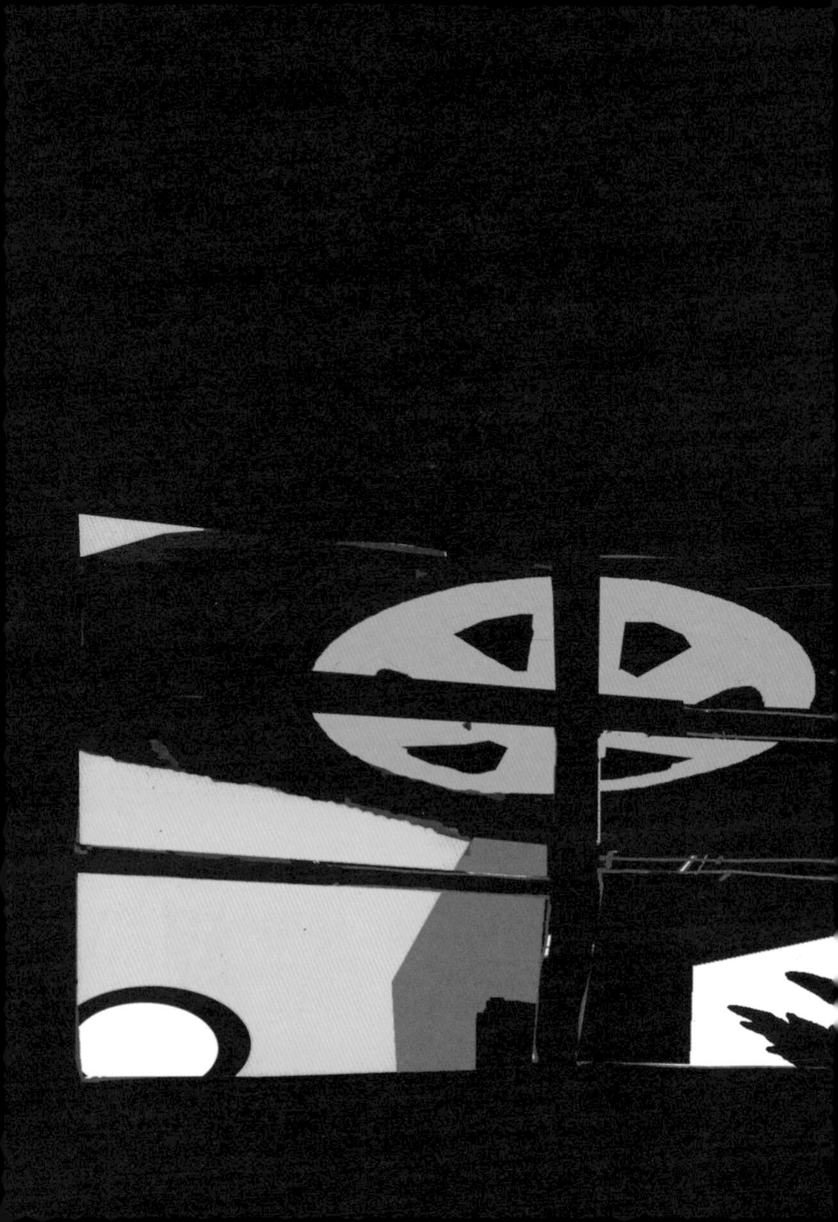

TRANSFORMING TRAVEL

CHAPTER 7

TRANSFORMING TRAVEL

We're in a pickle, travel-wise. Everybody wants to be somewhere else, at the same time. It isn't working.

MOTOR MADNESS

Cars are the ultimate Groan invention, enabling the operator to travel hundreds of miles on his or her large Groanish behind, without expending more energy than it takes to change a CD. Yes, cars Make Life Easy. And the carrying capacity allows you to get More, Cheaper.

For children, old people, hedgehogs and the rest of the non-driving universe, cars are a nightmare.

Quick Car Quiz

1. How many cars are there on British roads?
  a. 15 million **b.** 22 million **c.** 30 million

2. About how many people are killed or seriously

injured on British roads each year?
a. 40,000 **b.** 20,000 **c.** 60,000

3. What group are most at risk? **a.** Drivers **b.** Child
pedestrians and cyclists **c.** Motorcyclists

4. Who used to inhabit the space now taken up by
parked cars?

Answers: 1c. 2a. 3b. 4 children.

And what if everyone has a car? At the moment about
70% of people in Britain own cars, and the roads are
jammed solid at rush hour. Our cities are on the verge
of Gruesome Gridlock, but people keep buying more
cars. If you have one, why shouldn't I? And why not
have two or three? In America, the four-car family is
not unusual. In twenty years' time, there could be
more cars in Britain than people.

We're not going to get rid of cars overnight, but
suppose we use them less. We might burn less carbon,
use less oil, and make the roads quieter and safer for
cyclists and walkers.

Unfortunately your Groans have been driving so
long they've forgotten what legs are for, so it's up to
you to persuade them. Here are some suggestions:

Cut Down Your Car Miles

1. Combine journeys. If you're going to the dentist on the other side of town, think what else you could do at the same time (No, not while you're in the chair with your mouth open).

2. Once a week, ride a bike or take a bus or train to work. Then twice a week, and so on.

3. Share journeys by taking a neighbour to the shops (but remember to bring them back).

4. Have stuff delivered. A van doing the rounds is more efficient than you.

5. Instead of driving out of town at the weekend, see where you can go by train.

6. Walk to the shops once a week. A local butcher, baker, greengrocer and hardware store will have most of the stuff you need. And you might meet someone interesting, or even have a conversation – how often does that happen at the supermarket?

BIKES ARE BEST

The first bikes were pretty weird, but once people realised you didn't need to have one huge wheel and one tiny one, the whole world went bike mad. A hundred years ago, even fifty years ago, bikes filled the streets. In the Second World War, the Japanese army invaded Singapore by bike. There has never been a more efficient machine.

Funky Bike Facts

1. 18 bikes can park in the same space as one car.
2. In motion, 30 bikes take up the same space as one car.
3. If 40,000 people needed to coss a bridge in one hour, by train they'd need two lanes, by bus four lanes, by car twelve lanes, but by bike one lane.
4. Riding a bike makes you super fit and healthy, as long as you don't get splattered all over the road.

Unfortunately, fast-moving traffic and bikes don't mix well, so the more people drive, the more dangerous the roads become for cyclists, which means they drive instead, and it goes on. To break the Sinister Spiral of Car Dependency, you need to train your Groans.

THE PLANE TRUTH ABOUT FLYING

You know the story of Daedalus and Icarus? Dad makes wings. Son gets over-excited and flies too close to sun. Wings melt and fall to pieces. Son plummets to death. Moral: THINK CAREFULLY BEFORE LEAVING TERRA FIRMA.

In the old days, flying used to be dangerous and expensive, but now it's safe and cheap, and Groans love it. They love buzzing over to Paris or Prague for the weekend, and because everyone else is doing it too, they assume it must be A Good Thing. Of course, people used to feel like that about sending little boys up chimneys and putting little girls in charge of dangerous machinery.

The trouble with flying is that it uses an amount of energy way out of proportion to the benefit gained, i.e. a Groan lying by a pool or trawling around the shops. And there are Hidden Costs.

Stonehenge

Take Stonehenge. I don't mean literally. Just as an example. Not so long ago, you could wander among the stones, but now there's a huge fence round them. Why?

1. Because otherwise the stones might escape?

2. Because a gang of dastardly international criminals is planning to steal them?

3. Because so many people come to
see them that if there wasn't a
fence, the stones would be worn
away like the noses of cathedral
saints?

BRITISH
PEOPLE TOOK
234 MILLION
FLIGHTS IN
2006

A trip abroad used to be a rare
adventure, but now you just drive to
the airport, hop on a plane and hire a car. Groans
grumble about how they used to walk round
Stonehenge but they want to go everywhere and see
everything. They want More, Cheaper.

So Stonehenge is now hidden by a giant car park
full of coaches and a fence, and none of you will ever
see the old stones sitting quietly on the grass.

DON'T BE FOOLED BY BIOFUEL

Car owners, manufacturers and petrol companies are
always looking for ways to seem Green, and biofuels
are the New Big Thing. Instead of powering cars with
the energy from long-dead plants (i.e. oil), biofuels are
made from plants grown for the purpose – crops such
as wheat, oilseed rape and oil palms. The idea is that
the growing plants consume as much CO_2 as the car
engines will emit, but does this make biofuels Green?
Not in the slightest. So how can you be a Green driver?
By riding a bike instead.

CHAPTER 8

HOW TO TURN YOUR GARDEN GREEN

Do you have a garden? If so, what's it like?

1. Neat and Tidy with a nice trim lawn, nice trim roses, tomato plants in growbags (in summer, obviously) and a nice new fence.

2. A bit neglected, with ivy growing in the corner, a flower bed that needs some attention and more dandelion than grass in the 'lawn'.

3. A veritable jungle of bushes and shrubs, with plants that just started growing one day, insane creepers and a crazy old apple tree your Dad is meaning to cut down.

4. Decking. A patio heater. A pot.

If your garden is like Number 3, then you are doing Mother Nature a service. Fifty years of farming according to the Groan Philosophy of More, Cheaper has turned our countryside into a desert. It still looks green, but it's really grey. Birds, butterflies and bugs have disappeared en masse. It's like Rachel Carson (see Chapter Two, p10) predicted: Groans are waging war on everything wild.

Do you want your kids to grow up in a world where hedgehogs are a memory and you have to DOWNLOAD BIRDSONG? Wild plants and creatures need you to make your garden Green.

RETURN OF THE POISSON PATROL

Groans have two weapons in their war against Nature:

Poissons
They use weedkiller, bug spray, etc, to get rid of plants and creepy-crawlies they don't like. Unfortunately, it's like hiring a very stupid, trigger-happy assassin, since the poisons kill ladybirds, hoverflies and other useful insects, as well as annoying ones like greenfly.

Fertilisers
They use fertiliers to help their favourite plants grow. These are usually phosphates or nitrates, and they're also indiscriminate: when they get washed out of your garden into a stream or river, they can create an Algal Bloom, which sounds like a favourite great aunt but isn't. It's a big clump of green slime which feeds on fertilisers, gets huge, starves the water of oxygen and kills off other plants, fish, frogs, etc.

The scariest products contain both poison and fertiliser. They're called things like Weed'n'Feed. Find them. Make your parents get rid of them. Your garden doesn't need them, and neither does anyone else's.

COOL COMPOST, OR HOW TO PROFIT FROM MANKY OLD VEGETABLES

Compost is Cool. OK, so it's also yucky, smelly and full of worms and slugs, but the yuckiness is in a good cause. It can help you turn Manky Old Vegetables into Cash. But first, a story...

THE STORY OF PETE

About 2,500 years ago Pete was born. He endured a short, miserable life. He died, probably murdered in some brutal fashion by his best pals. But there his story does not end, because Pete was buried in a wet, acid soil, and his body was preserved like a pickled onion. Yes, Pete was buried in peat. Cut to the present and here are the Groans heading off to the Garden Centre to buy a growbag, which is a bit of peat wrapped in plastic.

Peat bog is a unique habitat, but Groans see peat as something that needs to be dug up, wrapped in plastic and used to grow a tomato plant. In its natural state, peat is rich, moist and full of nutrients, but wrapped in plastic it dries out, and pretty soon growbag and dead plant end up in the bin.

96%
OF OUR NATIVE PEAT BOGS HAVE BEEN DUG UP

But each Spring, Mum and Dad tell themselves they're going to do better, and so home they come with a growbag or two. What they don't suspect is that they might not be buying just peat – there might be a bit of Pete in there too. Pete has many brothers, also called Pete, and though archaeologists have rescued some of them, most get carved up by the giant peat-digging machines and then wrapped up in... my, that's quite a tomato plant you've got there, Mr Groan!

Compost has the same tomato plant-friendly properties as peat, but you make it in your back garden. Save vegetable scraps, shreds of newspaper and cardboard, old fruit (not citrus), egg shells, grass and weeds, etc, and chuck them in the Dalek shaped bin you can get from the Council. You keep piling the stuff in and it keeps disappearing. Leave it a year and you can start digging the rich black, non-stinky soil out of the bottom. Then find out the price of a growbag and charge the parents 10p less for a potful mixed half and half with plain old soil. They'll think they're getting a deal. Especially if you've told Mum the Pete story a few times.

QUICK GUIDE TO GARDEN CHEMICALS

Herbicide, pesticide, fungicide, insecticide, molluscicide, fungicide, rodenticide, hedgehogicide, froggicide, kitticide, babybirdicide, countrysidicide, Earthicide.

THE HUNGRY CATERPILLAR

Before lawnmowers were invented you had to be very rich to have a lawn, because you needed an army of servants snipping the grass with scissors. You had to cut grass and weeds with a scythe or a sickle, using your own muscle power. Dads in those days were brawny (and a bit sweaty). A garden used to be a place to relax and listen to the birds singing. Now you're more likely to hear the noise of Dad blowing away leaves or showing some weeds who's boss.

Imagine you're a peacock butterfly: you fly around looking for somewhere to lay eggs, find a nice patch of nettles and lay your eggs nearby, congratulating yourself on a job well done. A little later, caterpillars hatch, wriggly and hungry, and look around for their favourite type of food.

Oh dear, Dad's taken them all out with his new, heavy-duty strimmer (and probably killed a few hedgehogs too). No nettle, no caterpillar, no butterfly to land on the flowers Mum's planted to attract them.

Greener alternatives to Dad's Macho Machines

1. For fallen leaves, use a rake.

2. For weeds, use shears.

3. For slimy surfaces, use water and a brush.

4. For hedges, use clippers.

Still, better a Neat and Tidy garden than the wasteland of decking. What is it about Groans and decking? Do they think the house is about to up anchor and sail off round the world? Or do they love the fact that decking gets horribly slimy, so they have to spray it with high-pressure hoses and douse it with chemicals to get the slime off, and the chemicals run off into the soil and make what's left of the garden a toxic death zone?

Some creatures do love desks, though. The kind of creatures that love nasty wet slimy corners. Slugs and snails love a good deck, or even your Dad's terrible DIY deck, but frogs, thrushes and other predators don't.

HIDEOUS PATIO HEATERS

Do Groans really want the atmosphere to heat up? If they don't, why do they buy devices specifically designed to heat up the atmosphere? Budding eco-warriors! If your Groans have a patio heater, make them put it in the garage! If they insist on using it, scream loudly until they stop!

NICE BUTT

Next time that the Groans are at the Garden Centre looking at the complete garden irrigation system with 200 miles of hose, four remote controlled sprinkler systems and infra-red moisture sensors, point out that they can save themselves zillions of pounds and save loads of water by purchasing a water butt and watering can.

WATCH OUT FOR WATER WASTERS!

Water is precious, and wasting it isn't even fun. Here are the fines for water wasters:

OFFENCE	FINE	PAYABLE
Using a hose instead of a watering can	20p	On the spot
Leaving tap on while brushing teeth*	20p	On the spot
Use of poissonous cleaners	50p	Monthly
Buying non-recycled toilet paper	20p	On the spot**
Not fixing dripping taps	50p	Monthly
Failure to run washing machine on Eco setting	20p	On the spot
Ditto dishwasher	20p	On the spot
Excessively long shower or revoltingly deep bath	20p	On the spot

Plus compulsory course in Tap Turning. I mean, how hard is it to turn a tap on and off, for heaven's sake??!

**Refers to time of purchase, not usage.*

APPROVED

HOW TO TURN YOUR
TEACHERS GREEN

CHAPTER 9

HOW TO TURN YOUR TEACHERS GREEN

Schools are not known for being Green. After all, you go to school to learn stuff and become a Good Citizen, not to save the planet. Right? The trouble is, modern schools guzzle energy, puffing out CO_2 and undoing all the good work you've done at home, so you have no choice but to Turn Them Green.

GLORIOUS GREEN GOALS

Under the aegis* of your School Council, set up an Eco Team, with an Eco Monitor in each class. They can ask kids to suggest some Glorious Green Goals, which could be sensible ideas such as Cut Energy Use By 10%, or slightly loonier schemes. Then the Eco Team picks the best ten, prints them, and sends them to everyone: headteacher, governors, parents, caretaker.

*No, I'm not sure either, but it sounds great.

The Electric Classroom

Teachers used to keep warm in winter by vigorously writing on blackboards with squeaky chalk and throwing board dusters at inattentive children. Interactive whiteboards use electricity instead of teacher power, and then there are laptops, photocopiers, ICT suites and all the rest. What's to be done?

1. Post witty reminders next to each light switch and next to computers, etc, saying things like 'Help! Switch Me Off!'

2. Replace nasty old lightbulbs with Glorious Low Energy Bulbs.

3. Punish and reward.

Is your Classroom a Gruesome Greenhouse? Describe your classmates on a winter afternoon...

1. Alert, full of brilliant ideas, wrapped up in a jumper but with no signs of frostbite?

2. Huddled, shivering, like penguins on an iceberg?

3. Red-faced, sweating, and incapable of stringing a sentence together?

Answers: 1. *Lucky people – you probably have a thermostat and it's set to a pleasant 20 degrees;* 2. *The most unlikely scenario, unless you've time-travelled to the 1950s;* 3. *Time for action...*

1. Send a letter to parents in November saying: 'It's getting cold, for Heaven's sake, so jolly well send your children to school with a sweater and a proper coat. We're not going to make the polar bears homeless just because you can't be bothered to dress your children properly!' Alternatively, start a knitting club. Or crocheting.

2. Find a Groovy Green Governor to help you carry out an Energy Audit. Ensure the heating system has a thermostat. Even better, campaign for thermostats in individual classrooms. Keep the temperature at 20 degrees or below.

Schools rubbish! Er... School's rubbish! No... Schools' rubbish!

I never did understand apostrophe's. Anyway, the point is, schools need to shape up when it comes to rubbish and recycling. Here are some ideas:

1. Make paper recycling bins that are so stylish the cool kids hover around them, pretending to recycle

paper, and put one in each classroom, and get an adult to contact the council to arrange a paper pick-up.

AT 8.50AM IN TERM-TIME. 1 IN 5 CARS ON THE ROAD IS TAKING A KID TO SCHOOL

2. Get a compost bin while you're at it and fill with fruit peel, weeds, etc (see How to Turn Your Garden Green, Chapter 8, P65).

School Run or School Walk?

How often do you go to school? Two hundred times a year or so? It's a journey you do so much, you probably don't think about it, but the so-called School Run (actually a School Sit and Look Out the Window) causes more traffic congestion than anything else.

1. Have a competition: see who can come up with the most inventive way of getting to school. Better still, make it an art project. Think bike, roller skates, wheelies, scooter, donkey, pony and trap, glider, Tardis, winged horse, back of a dolphin…

2. Organise a monthly No Car Day, for teachers and kids. Make it competitive, with Green prizes for the best class, and Sensational Stickers.

Playground Pleasures: How would you describe your school grounds?

1. A beautiful green park with gracious willows, a little pond and scrubby bits for wildlife.

2. An expanse of grey tarmac.

3. Mostly b. with a hint of a. here and there.

Time for another art project: My Vision for a Glorious Green Playground

1. Set no limits: You could plant a wood and have ropewalks high up in the trees, or bring in bricks and wood and use them to build huts and shelters.

2. Count bugs: Get everyone looking in corners and under stones. Find out what creatures and plants share your school, and come up with plans to encourage more.

3. Dig up some tarmac and make a vegetable garden.

In Your Lunchbox: Loads of kids take a packed lunch. What's in yours?

1. A sandwich. A drink. An apple.

2. Seventy-three kinds of plastic packaging containing Cheesy Sluggits, Wiffle Bars, Nibbies and other Sinister Snacks that are more entertainment than foodstuff.

3. Nothing, because you're looking forward to a wholesome, Jamie Oliver-style school dinner. Or turkey twizzlers and chips.

4. All your favourite foods: organic carrots, homegrown baby tomatoes, sliced pepper, hummous, a Fairtrade banana, home-made flapjack – packed in reusable containers.

HOW TO TURN YOUR TEACHERS GREEN

You know teachers have a tough life, filling your heads with info like $c=2\pi r$ and Henry VIII's wives, having their Ofsteds inspected etc. They don't need harassing about switching lights off. But you still need to turn them Green.

To help you, here's a well-kept secret

about teachers: They're no different from the rest of us. They like to do well. They like a little appreciation. They want to be Green, but, like the rest of us, they find it a bit of a struggle. In particular, teachers suffer from one dreadfully Groanish addiction...

LAMENTABLE LAMINATING

Don't teachers just love to laminate? Nothing pleases them more than to take biodegradable, recyclable paper and cover it in a layer of plastic. Why?!

1. They want to leave a mark on the world.

2. They think kids don't notice anything unless it's wrapped in plastic.

3. They like to feel special.

Your teachers will Green up in an instant if you make them feel good. How? Reward them with certificates they can put on the fridge and stickers for their bikes and badges they can wear with pride. Give a teacher a nice green badge made of recycled cardboard with the words 'Green Teacher' on it and they will never need to laminate again.

But remember, these are grown-ups you're dealing with, not kids, so you don't have to be nice when they fail dismally. Feel free to hold a monthly competition to see who is Green and who is Groan, and display the results prominently.

Does your teacher:

1. Switch lights, computers, etc, off when not in use?

2. Use paper on both sides then recycle?

3. Keep the heat at a healthy 20 degrees?

4. Say no to Lamentable Laminating?

INSPIRATIONAL IDEAS FOR A GLORIOUS GREEN FUTURE

Why not put your DT lessons to good use: thinking up ways to make a Greener world? Sometimes a little thing can have a big impact.

How about:

1. A way of capturing methane in class after lunch?

2. A tiny hydroelectric turbine that can generate electricity from water running down a drainpipe?

3. Sinister Snacks that eat their own packaging?

4. A new power system, based on kids pedalling as they work?

HOW TO BE A GREEN
CITIZEN

CHAPTER 10

HOW TO BE A GREEN CITIZEN

More and more people are turning Green: you'll find Greens in the classroom, Greens at the farmers' market, Greens at the library, Greens selling solar lamps and Green paint (other colours available on demand), Greens fishing bikes out of rivers and managing woods while the dormice snooze.

Everywhere Greens are trying to undo the damage caused by those Grumbly Groans: campaigning against road building schemes and airports, and for local railways. For the budding Eco-Warrior, there are loads of organisations and groups to join, from Friends of the Earth and Greenpeace to wildlife charities and local groups that devote their time to a particular patch of land or stretch of stream.

Keep your Eyes Open

1. Use your eyes (and nose) to check for pollution in streams and ponds: if the water stinks or the fish are all belly up, tell your local Council.

2. Report piles of rubbish or abandoned shopping trolleys.

3. Keep checking the labels in the supermarket.

4. Be alert to Greenwash*.

No, not a fabulous laundry detergent. Greenwash is what businesses do to make them seem Green. The most obvious example is painting a petrol station so it looks like a field.

BE AN I-GREEN

Email is a wonderful thing. Your voice or handwriting might identify you as a Younger Member of Society, but nobody will guess your age from an email. You can write to newspapers, complain to the Council, take part in planning protests and express your opinions on consumer websites and forums, just the same as an adult. And why not? It's your world, after all.

THE BOY WHO SAVED THE SEVERN BEACH LINE

Britain once had an amazing railway network. You could go practically anywhere by train, which was great for people who didn't have a car or a horse or, er, a steam engine. Then, in the 1960s, the government decided life would be better if everyone drove cars, and set about closing a third of the network – mostly the branch lines used by schoolkids and shoppers.

But when officials released figures saying the Severn Beach Line in Bristol was used by too few people a teenager went out and counted passengers. He proved that the figures were wrong, and forty years later the trains are still trundling.

RADICAL RIDERS

Local councils like to boast about how many miles of cycle lane they've created, because it makes them look Green, but they don't like to upset motorists. So they put in a hundred metres of lane where it fits easily, then, when the road gets narrow and you're in mortal danger of being squidged by a lorry, take it away again.

It's up to you to make a fuss. If you come across a suicidal cycle lane, make a note of where it is and email the council. Tell your local cycle group, if there is one. Write to the paper. Tell them you Could Have Been Killed, for Heaven's Sake.

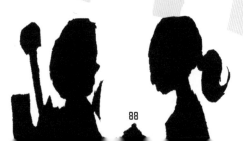

HOW TO DEFEAT DASTARDLY DEVELOPERS

You probably know all about the Housing Boom – a truly Groanish waste of time and energy. It will all end in tears sometime soon, but in the meantime Dastardly Developers are trying to cram as many Hideous Houses and Frightful Flats as they can into every spare bit of space, so they can sell them for a fortune.

They think empty space is a waste of space, but you know that it isn't. You know that allotments, lanes, forgotten scrubby patches and bits of waste ground are necessary and important. They're a vital habitat for wildlife – hedgehogs, birds, butterflies, frogs. They're somewhere quiet where people can walk dogs and ponder the mysteries of existence (or whether to have mushy peas with their fish and chips). They're places where you can hang out with your friends.

Unfortunately, no planning officer will listen to a bunch of kids arguing that their unofficial football pitch is more valuable than a new housing development, but there are ways and means. You could join a local protest group, if there is one, and get your Groans to join too; explain that your schoolwork will suffer if you lose your space; look for interesting or unusual wildlife and tell local Green groups about them – many a development has been halted by a rare newt! You can also contact the media and explain that you and your friends are in danger of becoming obese and anti-social, if you lose your cherished patch.

Be an Awkward Customer

1. Leave packaging at the supermarket checkout
2. Complain about supermarkets importing apples in October, when British apples are falling off the trees.
3. Inspect plastic packaging. Does it carry a recycling symbol? If so, can you actually recycle it, or is this more of a theoretical thing? If the only place you can recycle it is some place out on the Isle of Wight, make a fuss.

LIVE GREEN

The future of the world is in your hands. OK, so there are a few billion other people with a say in it too, but your choices and actions will affect the course of history as much as anyone else's.

However, your parents live their lives, you are free to choose your own course. Which is it to be:

Groan or Green?

1. Do you want to fill gaps in the land or the recycling bank?

2. Do you want people to suffer in the cause of your cheap stuff, or to live comfortably like you?

3. Do you want to watch life on TV, or take part in it?

4. Do you always want to listen to music on an MP3 player, or learn an instrument and play it yourself?

5. Do you want to experience the world through a car window, or at your own pace, under your own power?

6. Do you want hedgehogs and bumblebees to disappear, or to flourish?

7. Do you want Ghastly Global Warming to keep getting worse, or would you rather do something about it?

Of course, it isn't easy being Green. We're only human, after all. But if you follow Groan philosophy you'll be unhappy, stressed, overweight and, quite probably, under water.

So instead of More, Cheaper!
LESS, BETTER!
Instead of Make Life Easy!
MAKE LIFE FUN!

FOR MORE GREAT TITLES
FROM TANGENT BOOKS VISIT
WWW.TANGENTBOOKS.CO.UK